National Museums Scotland

in Tir

Fran

CW01506590

SCOTTIES SERIES EDITORS
Frances and Gordon Jarvie

Contents

Published in Great Britain in 2010
by NMS Enterprises Limited – Publishing
a division of NMS Enterprises Limited
National Museums Scotland
Chambers Street, Edinburgh EH1 1JF

Text © Frances Jarvie and Gordon Jarvie 2010

Images (for © see below and on page 40)

ISBN: 978-1-905267-34-7

British Library Cataloguing in Publication Data
A catalogue record of this book
is available from the British Library.

Book design concept by Redpath.
Cover design and image work by Mark
Blackadder.

Layout by NMSE – Publishing.
Printed and bound in the United Kingdom by
Bell & Bain Limited, Glasgow.

CREDITS

*Thanks are due to the following individuals and
organisations who have supplied images and
photographs for this publication.*

*Every attempt has been made to contact copy-
right holders to use the material in this publication.
If any image has been inadvertently missed, please
contact the publisher.*

COVER

'The Mauchline Holy Fair' by Alexander Carse,
c.1830 (Reproduced by kind permission of The
National Trust for Scotland/photo: John Sinclair)
Engraving of Robert Burns after Nasmyth, from
CASSELL'S *OLD AND NEW EDINBURGH: Its
History, its People, and its Places* by James
Grant (Cassell & Co: London, n.d.)

TEXT

NATIONAL MUSEUMS SCOTLAND
(© National Museums Scotland)
for pages 4 (interior & Burns' Cottage postcard);
5 (grandparents by W. Geikie, from *Etchings
Illustrative of Scottish Character* by Sir Thomas
Dick Lauder & 'Carron Ironworks from Falkirk');
6 (Mount Oliphant); 7 (Watt's gear system); 8
(bowl & harvesting oats); 9 (kitchen utensils &

Keiller label); 10 (flax spinning wheel & harvest-
ing); 11 (Galloway funeral by John Copland &
John Paul Jones' watch); 13 (Lunardi and Tytler
& Mauchline Ware); 14 (route map of Slave
Trade); 16 (New Town plan); 17 (Canongate
Church); 20 (bone chanter and reel music); 23
('A Musical Souter', W. Geikie, from *Etchings
Illustrative of Scottish character* by T. Dick Lauder
& Tam o' Shanter at the inn, from *Illustrated
Songs of Robert Burns*); 26 (pistol); 32 (*Original
Scottish Airs for the Voice*, ed. G. Thomson,
1822); 37 (replica of plough); 38 (scene from
Alloway Kirk from *Illustrated Songs of Robert
Burns*); 39 (Maggie loses her tail, *Illustrated
Songs of Robert Burns*); activities section pages
iii (etching) and v (famous Scots)

FURTHER CREDITS (see activities section, p. viii).

SCOTTIE BOOKS

For a full listing of NMS Enterprises
Limited – Publishing titles and related
merchandise:

www.nms.ac.uk/books

Ayr and Surrounding Area

Burns' Family Tree

William Burness = Agnes Brown
(1721-84)   (1732-1820)

Robert Burns = Jean Armour   Gilbert   Annabella   John   Isabella
(1759-96)   (1765-1834)   (1760-1827)   (1764-1832)   (1769-85) (1771-1858)
                                     Agnes   William
                                   (1762-1834)   (1767-90)

Robert   Jean   Twin   Francis   William   Elizabeth   James   Maxwell
(1786-1857) (1786-87)   daughters   Wallace   Nicol   Riddell   Glencairn   (1796-99)
                         (unnamed)   (1789-1803)   (1791-1872) (1792-95)   (1794-1865)
                         (1788)

Illegitimate children of the poet:

— Elizabeth ('Bess') Burns
(1785-1816)
mother: Elizabeth ('Betsey') Paton

— Robert Burns
(1788-)
mother: Janet ('Jenny') Clow

— Elizabeth ('Betty') Burns
(1791-1873)
mother: Ann Park

Family ties

Apart from two brothers, the rest of Robert's brothers and sisters lived well into the next century.

Isabella, Robert's youngest sister, is pictured here. She married John Begg in 1793.

Maybole and Alloway

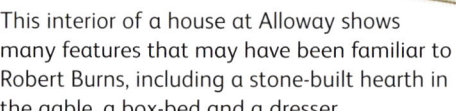

'I was born a very poor man's son.'
Robert Burns

William Burness (later Burns) met Agnes Brown at a fair in the High Street of Maybole. William, a market-gardener, built a clay cottage with turfed roof, living-room, kitchen and byre, in nearby Alloway for his wife, when they married in December 1757. Just over a year later, on 25 January 1759, their son Robert was born in the now world-famous cottage. Ten days later, in a howling gale, the gable end collapsed. Robert was hurriedly taken to stay at a neighbour's house.

This interior of a house at Alloway shows many features that may have been familiar to Robert Burns, including a stone-built hearth in the gable, a box-bed and a dresser.

Despite this stormy beginning, Robert's father rebuilt the cottage and was determined his growing family would be taught some skills other than farming. Robert's mother Agnes had a fine singing voice for old ballads. From an early age, this inspired Burns in his love of Scottish folk music. There was also an older relative, Betty Davidson, who helped Agnes in the cottage and small dairy. She was an expert storyteller – especially of scary tales about 'devils, ghosts, fairies, brownies, witches, warlocks, spunkies, kelpies, elf-candles, dead-lights … [and] apparitions'.

BURNS' COTTAGE. AYR.

Alloway

This postcard of Burns' cottage in Alloway, Ayr, is dated *c*.1910. In 1900 a museum was built at the back of the cottage. The humble cottage enabled people to imagine Burns as an inspired ploughman.

A young tutor, John Murdoch, was employed for Robert, aged seven, and his younger brother Gilbert. Five families shared the cost of the tutor, with each family in turn providing Murdoch with board over the year. Reading, spelling, grammar, the Bible, poetry, arithmetic and church music were all taught enthusiastically by the tutor.

Robert was to grow up at a time of great change in the daily life of people in Britain and William Burness patiently prepared his children. Before 1760 more than 94 per cent of adults earned their living on the land, with six per cent making goods. But steampower, new inventions in cloth-making and coal-mining were soon to change the countryside forever. The time known as the **Industrial Revolution** was about to arrive.

Timeline

1759   Robert Burns is born on 25 January in Alloway, Ayrshire.

Carron Ironworks opens at Falkirk. Using local coal and iron ore, it was famous for its production of steam engines, carronades (or guns) used by Horatio Nelson's navy, and the first iron plough – all part of the **Industrial Revolution**.

1760   George III becomes king.

1763   France cedes Canada to Britain.

Swing plough (or Scots plough) is invented by James Small, a metal plough that could be pulled by two horses. It replaced the old wooden plough.

1765   Robert and his brother Gilbert begin their schooling at home, under tutor John Murdoch.

Right: King George III.

Below, left: Learning under the guidance of grand-parents, 18th century.

Below: Carron Ironworks, seen from Falkirk, c.1790.

Mount Oliphant: a moorland farm

'Poor tenant bodies, scant o' cash ...'   from 'The Twa Dogs'

Aged seven, Robert Burns and family moved to a farm two miles from Alloway at Mount Oliphant. His father William became a tenant farmer, paying rent to a factor – usually raising the money with great difficulty. Formal schooling ended at age nine, as Robert had to learn to work the plough.

The whole family toiled to get some results from the very poor soil at Mount Oliphant. There was no cash to make improvements, such as planting hedges, shelter belts, or rotating the crops. Their diet was, as a result, very poor. As Robert's brother Gilbert later wrote, 'For several years butcher's meat was a stranger in the house'.

Yet William Burness continued to strive for his children. In 1772 Robert and Gilbert studied in Dalrymple on alternate weeks, since they could not be spared from the farm at the same time. By 15 years old, Robert was the main labourer on the farm. Everything had to be done by hand and it was heavy work. This caused a strain on his heart, which was never to leave him. There were now seven children in the family to be fed from the land.

Springtime was the ploughing season. Robert took great pride in his skill with a plough. A horse-drawn harrow levelled the soil before seeds were sown by hand. At harvest time,

Below: Mount Oliphant in more recent times. The land has been carefully drained since Burns' day, when it was wretched and heavy to work. No wonder it affected the health of the young Robert.

Mount Oliphant

scythes and sickles were used to cut the grain. It was then flailed to separate grain from the stalks, and winnowed to remove the chaff from the grain. During one harvest Robert found himself working alongside Nelly Kirkpatrick, who sang as she worked. It was to her favourite reel that he composed his first song, 'Handsome Nell' – 'done, when my heart glowed with honest, warm simplicity'. His passion for writing had begun.

Website watch

Burns was deeply impressed by the **American Revolution** of 1776. Scotland's **Declaration of Arbroath** in 1320 (pictured above) was a letter written to the Pope, and it may have been read by those who drafted the United States Declaration of Independence. It stated that in Scotland the 'people' are supreme, rather than the monarch or parliament.

Go to **Declaration of Arbroath** at **www.bbc.co.uk/history/scottishhistory/ media_museum** under **Wars of Independence**

Timeline

1766   James Craig wins a competition to design the New Town of Edinburgh.

1769-70   The sea captain James Cook investigates the east coast of Australia after charting New Zealand.

1770   Potatoes are now the main item of diet in the Highlands and Islands.

1774   James Watt and Matthew Boulton manufacture patented steam engines.

1776   Adam Smith publishes *The Wealth of Nations*, the first modern work on economics.

         On 4 July, 13 British colonies of North America make a Declaration of Independence from British rule.

Below: James Watt's famous 'sun and planet' gear system was suitable for driving machinery as well as pumping water. The wheels moved around each other like a planet orbiting the sun.

Some hae meat: food in the 1700s

'The halesome porritch, chief of Scotia's food …'

from 'The Cotter's Saturday Night'

Food had to be hearty and honest if you were working on the land. Broth, porridge, skirlie (onion and oatmeal) and stovies made the best of local produce – as we see again today at farmers' markets. The diet slowly improved throughout the century as farming methods changed.

Oats, barley, and later wheat, were the main cereals. Oats was the most versatile – it was made into oatcakes, bannocks, brose and porridge, but not bread or pastry. Bread, as we know it, was only baked in the towns from wheat flour, but was too pricey for ordinary folk. Barley was mainly used for brewing ale, drunk in preference to water.

A glazed earthenware bowl inscribed with Burns' 'Selkirk Grace'. It was probably made by the Cumnock Pottery, East Ayrshire in the late 19th century.

Dairy produce, such as butter, cheese and milk, was essential for a balanced diet. Burns kept Galloway cows at Ellisland farm and Ayrshire Dunlop is still a distinctive Cheddar-type cheese.

Until potatoes and turnips were introduced, vegetables were mostly onions, leeks and kail (a kind of green-leaf vegetable known as colewort). At first turnips were thought to be a delicacy and were kept in the fruit bowl! However, it was potatoes that became a staple part of the diet in winter.

Harvesting oats

A crofter cutting an oat crop with a scythe, Shetland, 1970s.

As for fruit – well, there were brambles and wild raspberries to be picked from the hedgerows for free – and apples, pears and plums at the market. In the mid-1700s, however, eating raw fruit was not advised. Rhubarb was still thought of as a medicine, not as a food. If you fancied fish, there was an abundant supply of herring which was salted and smoked. Eating salmon, however, was considered 'common'!

As Burns' 'Selkirk Grace' states: '*Some* hae meat …'. It was only if a beast could not survive the winter that it was slaughtered. Meat was a rarity for most people and only wealthier folk ate it on a regular basis. Haggis was a common dish after a carcase had been sold: the intestines, kidney and liver were kept to be chopped up and mixed with oatmeal and oxblood.

To wash it all down there was milk and lots of ale. Tea-drinking also grew in popularity as the tax on this new import was reduced. Tea-leaves no longer had to be kept under lock and key! At the end of a long, hard day, the last cup of tea before bed was often mixed with a little whisky.

Right: Some of the kitchen utensils that may have been familiar to the Burness family.

Food facts

- It's official – porridge *is* good for you! Oats have anti-oxidant properties and help to reduce blood cholesterol.

- Another breakfast staple – marmalade – became a commercially-made commodity during the 1700s. When a Spanish ship laden with Seville oranges was forced by storms to tie up at Dundee Harbour, the cargo was sold off cheaply to James Keiller who ran a sweet and preserves shop in the Seagate, Dundee. His wife Janet came up with an orange version of quince (related to pear and apple) marmalade, and so began the world's first marmalade factory.

9

Lochlea and linen

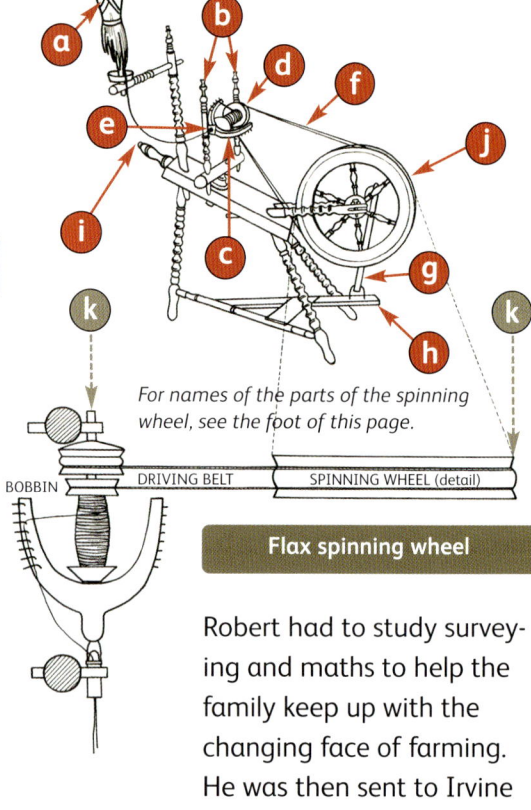

For names of the parts of the spinning wheel, see the foot of this page.

BOBBIN

DRIVING BELT

SPINNING WHEEL (detail)

Flax spinning wheel

'… like a true poet, not worth a sixpence …' Robert Burns

The final tenant farm for William Burness was at Lochlea, in the parish of Tarbolton. It was another battleground money-wise, with Robert's father taking the laird to court over broken promises on improvements. However, a new crop, flax (lint in Scotland), was being promoted by the Government, and farmers were paid extra to grow it. The textile industry was expanding and linen goods, made from flax, were woven in the villages. These skills were transferred easily to factories when cheaper cotton replaced the coarser linen towards the end of the 1700s.

Robert had to study surveying and maths to help the family keep up with the changing face of farming. He was then sent to Irvine to study 'lint dressing' – the long preparation of the flax that eventually produced linen thread. Robert had high hopes of leaving work as a farmer and took a share in a mill. However, disaster struck as the mill went up in flames and he was left penniless again.

Flax harvesting

Harvesting flax during the First World War.

Flax spinning wheel (see above):

a = **distaff**, with a bundle of flax in position
b = **maidens**, upright supports for the flyer and bobbin
c = **flyer**
d = **pirn, reel** or **bobbin**
e = the eye in the **spindle** through which the unspun fibre passes
f = **driving belt**   g = **driving rod**
h = **treadle, foot-plate** or **footboard**
i = **temper pin**   j = **wheel**
k = detail of part of machine from the **'bobbin' [d]** to **'wheel' [j]**

During his time at Lochlea, Burns formed the Tarbolton Bachelors' Club. The clubroom was in a pub – with a limit of 3d, or threepence, to be spent each night. The club was a debating society for unmarried men – and no doubt a lively one! Burns had also taken dancing lessons at Tarbolton, much against the wishes of his father.

Robert's writing continued, alongside farm-work, with the Ayrshire countryside and its people – especially the lassies – shaping his ideas for poems and songs. When Robert was 25, his exhausted father died. Robert now became head of the household and Lochlea was given up for another farm near Mauchline.

An 18th-century funeral in Galloway or Dumfriesshire, by artist John Copland.

Timeline

1778	Edinburgh is reputed to have 400 illicit whisky stills!
1779	Scots-born John Paul Jones, who became an American naval officer, targets Leith, Edinburgh's port, in the American War of Independence.
1780	Linen manufacture in Scotland vastly increased.
1780s	Disastrous harvests cause famine in the Scottish Highlands.
1783	Remaining American colonies are given their independence.
1784	William Tytler makes the first hot air balloon ascent in Scotland.
	William Burness dies and Robert becomes head of the household.

Website watch

Study for yourself the farming problems that were faced in the 1700s – and how people tried to solve them. Go to the section 'Working on Farms' at:

www.ltscotland.org.uk/scottishhistory/ industrialrevolution/dailylife

Right: The gravestone of Robert's father and mother in Alloway Kirk. Robert mourned deeply for his father, a man who had laboured hard in the fields, but who found time to read widely and pass his learning on to his family.

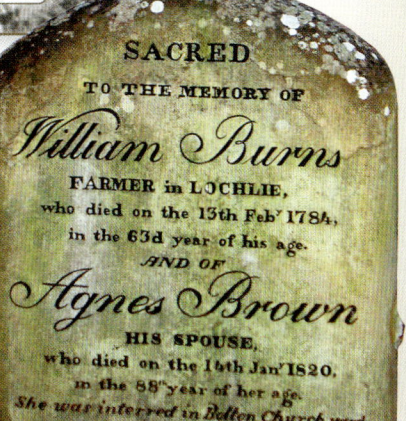

SACRED
TO THE MEMORY OF
William Burns
FARMER in LOCHLIE,
who died on the 13th Feb' 1784,
in the 63d year of his age.
AND OF
Agnes Brown
HIS SPOUSE,
who died on the 14th Jan' 1820,
in the 88" year of her age.
She was interred in Bolton Church yard
East Lothian.

Right: A silver pocket watch owned by the Scots-born naval officer John Paul Jones, inscribed with 'J.P.J.' on the back. John Paul Jones is credited with being the founder of the United States Navy. During the American War of Independence, he terrorised the coast of Scotland from the sea.

Rab Mossgiel

'I now began to be known in the neighbourhood as a maker of rhymes …' Robert Burns

Robert and his brother Gilbert rented Mossgiel farm, near Mauchline. (It was at this time that the family name was changed to Burns from Burness.) The farm was situated on high ground with early frosts and poor topsoil – and to make matters worse the brothers had bought bad seed. A late harvest with much of the crop lost meant that, after two years, Robert's share of the farm was transferred to Gilbert.

However, having farm servants for the first time gave Robert space to write some of his greatest poetry. Much of his work was composed in the loft, shared with Gilbert.

Fast fact

You can visit many of the places in Mauchline that feature in Burns' poems.

Take the **Burns Audio Trail**, starting at the **Burns House Museum**, to lead you around the sites.

Nicknamed 'Rab Mossgiel', Burns went nowhere without his writing materials. His poems 'To a Mountain Daisy' and 'To a Mouse' were written in the middle of ploughing. Other poems written at this time were 'The Jolly Beggars', 'The Cotter's Saturday Night', 'Holy Willie's Prayer' and 'The Twa Dogs'.

It was an intense period of writing genius, and handwritten copies of the poems were passed on to his friends, until demand called for them to be published. His first book of poems (the famous Kilmarnock edition), had a print run of 612 copies. It sold out within a month. Due to lack of funds, a further edition had to wait until Robert had visited Edinburgh. But a turbulent time lay ahead for the poet.

Left: It was in 1785 that Ayrshire cows began to be farmed throughout the area. In this photograph, prime specimens are being lead by Bruce Wilson (far right) at a local agricultural show in the early 1960s, a tradition which continues to this day. The breed has changed little since 1785.

Vincenzo Lunardi (middle), offers his hand to fellow balloonist William Tytler (see Timeline on page 11) in this cartoon by John Kay.

Timeline

1784 Robert Burns meets Jean Armour in Mauchline.

1785 An Ayrshire breed of cow is farmed; and Dunlop cheese is developed.

Vincenzo Lunardi, the Italian balloonist, makes flights over Edinburgh and Glasgow.

1786 *Poems chiefly in the Scottish Dialect* is printed and published in Kilmarnock (31 July) (see opposite page).

Mail coaches travel between Edinburgh and London in 60 hours.

Did you know?

- A Mauchline company still makes the finest curling stones in the world. It has supplied curling stones for the last three Winter Olympic Games, made of 60-million-year-old granite from the island of Ailsa Craig, Firth of Clyde. Burns mentions the island in his poem 'Duncan Grey' – 'Meg was as deaf as Ailsa Craig'!

- Another company in Mauchline produced highly collectable wooden objects for domestic use – such as tea-caddies, boxes, photo-frames, and so on. Made from local wood, they were decorated with transfers, fern patterns or tartan.

Website watch

Burns had a lot to say about the **Industrial Revolution** and how it affected people and their environment.

Listen to the poem 'To a Mouse' at:

www.bbc.co.uk/history/scottishhistory/ media_museum

and go to the section on **Revolution**.

A scene from 'The Jolly Beggars', based on the painting by Sir William Allan RA in 1823.

Jamaica bound

'I had taken the last farewell of my few friends; my chest was on the way to Greenock; I had composed the last song I should ever measure in Caledonia ...'

Robert Burns

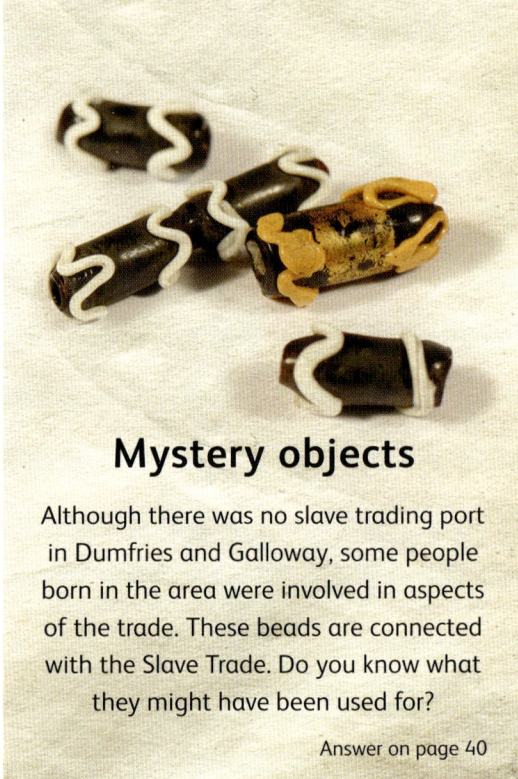

Mystery objects

Although there was no slave trading port in Dumfries and Galloway, some people born in the area were involved in aspects of the trade. These beads are connected with the Slave Trade. Do you know what they might have been used for?

Answer on page 40

Robert and Gilbert's farm at Mossgiel had been an unending struggle. Robert's rather complicated love life was in turmoil. He was still penniless, but hoped to marry a pregnant Jean Armour – whose father was horrified. He then fell in love with Margaret Campbell, his 'Highland Mary'. She went to Greenock

to wait for him, but caught typhus there and died from the illness.

Dr Patrick Douglas, a friend of Burns, had a share of a sugar plantation in Jamaica. He offered Burns a post there as book-keeper.

Below: A map of the 'triangular trade' route taken by slave-traders.

The Slave Trade

Find out more about the **Slave Trade** at the **National Maritime Museum** and use the interactive map:

www.nmm.ac.uk

Follow the interactive site

www.ltscotland.org.uk

and find out about the **Middle Passage**.

October is **Black History Month**. It is a month which highlights the role of black people in the history of modern Britain.

Many Jamaican estates were owned by Scots and farmed by slaves. Scottish ships left Glasgow laden with cargoes of cloth, guns, ammunition and glassware to barter with traders on the slave coast of West Africa. The ships then carried slaves to the West Indies on the second leg of their journey; and finally sailed back across the Atlantic to Scotland laden with sugar, rum and tobacco. This trade became known later as the 'Black Holocaust', because of the millions of slaves who died in transit.

But before Burns emigrated, there was a glimmer of hope for him. His collection of poems, written to raise money to emigrate, was a huge success. Printed in Kilmarnock as a subscription issue, word of it quickly spread to Edinburgh. Scotland's capital now wanted to meet the ploughman poet in person, so plans to emigrate were put on hold. Burns went to the Scottish capital instead.

This printed note is an invitation to subscribe to Burns' first collection of poems, later referred to as the **Kilmarnock edition**.

Highland Mary

Wi mony a vow, and lock'd embrace,
Our parting was fu' tender;
And, pledging aft to meet again,
We tore oursels asunder;
But, oh! fell Death's untimely frost,
That nipt my Flower sae early!
Now green's the sod, and cauld's the clay
That wraps my Highland Mary!

Margaret Campbell and Robert had exchanged bibles and vows of eternal love, but they were never to meet again.

Burns in Edinburgh

'At Edinburgh I was in a new world ...'   Robert Burns

The familiar sights of Edinburgh's Old Town. The Mercat Cross was a haven for traders, pedlars and merchants. *Mercat* is a Scots word for 'market'.

Burns came to Edinburgh partly because he wanted to travel, partly to promote his *Poems* to William Creech, bookseller. In those days Edinburgh was becoming a Jekyll and Hyde city, with two different sides to it. There was a medieval Old Town – colourful and smelly – where Burns stayed in Baxter's Close, off the Royal Mile. To the north, however, was the start of the elegant New Town, begun in 1767. The aristocracy and *literati* had now moved away from the cramped, squalid High Street, into splendid, roomy Georgian houses, laid out in fine rows and squares.

Edinburgh was now calling itself the 'Athens of the North'. It was not just a place of fine new classical buildings; it was also a power-house of intellectual activity. It was said that you could stand by the Mercat Cross and 'in a few minutes take fifty men of genius by the hand'.

Background: James Craig's completed plan of 1767 shows a move from the cramped and chaotic layout of the Old Town of Edinburgh to the regulated lines of the New Town.

On his first visit to the capital (November 1786 to May 1787), Burns was hailed almost like a celebrity, yet he was only 27. Everyone in Edinburgh society wanted to meet him, so he was invited frequently to the grand homes in the New Town. He was also welcomed by legal bigwigs at the newly-opened Assembly Rooms, and they subscribed to 100 copies of the new (second) edition of his poems.

William Creech, Bookseller

Creech was one of Edinburgh's leading bookseller publishers. His shop was beside the Mercat Cross at the Luckenbooths, beside St Giles High Kirk. From his shop door you could look down the canyon of the High Street towards the Forth and the fields of East Lothian beyond. Creech was a councillor and a bailie, but Burns thought him a bit of a 'holy willie' !

Robert Burns was encouraged to go to Edinburgh by James Cunningham, 13th Earl of Glencairn, who was a fan of his poetry. Through him, Burns became a popular figure among Edinburgh society and attended a number of literary salons.

While in Edinburgh, Burns paid for a grave-stone for Robert Fergusson, a fellow poet. He also spoke to 15-year-old Walter Scott (see page 18) at a society gathering.

From Edinburgh, the now celebrated Burns set off on a tour around the Scottish Borders in May 1787.

Canongate Church

THE GRAVE OF ROBERT FERGUSSON
In Canongate Church Yard

Canongate Churchyard, on Edinburgh's famous street – the Royal Mile – has many famous grave-stones marking the final resting-places of the great and good. Such worthies include the economist **Adam Smith**, the young poet **Robert Fergusson** and Burns' 'Clarinda' – **Mrs Agnes McLehose**. The beautiful song 'Ae Fond Kiss' was written especially for Mrs McLehose.

Tour of the Borders

'… braw, braw lads o'
Gala Water … '

from a song by Robert Burns

Melrose (the Abbey is pictured here) was just one stop of many on Burns' Border tour. He also visited the sites mentioned in the **Route finder** on the opposite page.

Imagine a landscape of few trees, strips instead of fields, muddy lanes, no railways, fences, hedges or wind farms. Few people left their own parish in their lifetime. Burns' world so far had been in Ayrshire, around Dumfries and in Edinburgh. Now he wanted to travel. It was his dream to see some of the famous sites around Scotland. The tour of the Scottish Borders was also undertaken to celebrate the second edition of his poems, printed by William Creech in Edinburgh.

Accompanied initially by a lawyer friend, Robert Ainslie, Burns set out for the Borders to collect local songs and their verses. Burns travelled on a mare called Jenny Geddes, named after the feisty woman who threw her stool at the preacher in St Giles High Kirk in 1637, sparking a riot.

An Edinburgh contact, music-seller James Johnson, had published volume 1 of *The Scots Musical Museum* in 1787. Burns worked for him on hundreds of old songs and tunes to

Walter Scott

Walter Scott (1771-1832) was just a boy when he encountered Robert Burns in Edinburgh in 1786. He saw Burns as 'strong and robust; his manners rustic, not clownish'. Scott himself would become a writer and antiquarian of great importance, writing such classics as *Rob Roy*, *The Heart of Midlothian* and *Ivanhoe*. Such was his fame that a monument was dedicated to him on Edinburgh's Princes Street in 1844.

Route finder

Find a good road map and plot the route Burns took from Edinburgh. Can you think of any famous sites Burns might have seen in the Borders? Suggestions on page 40

Edinburgh > Haddington > Gifford > Dunbar > Bilsdean > St Abbs > Eyemouth > Berwick > Duns > Coldstream > Cornhill-on-Tweed > Kelso > Jedburgh > Hawick > Selkirk > Bemersyde > St Boswells > Earlston > Melrose > Galashiels > Innerleithen > Peebles

add to later volumes of the collection. He improved some, re-wrote others, and even rearranged the music to fit. Burns was becoming a folk hero. His songs have inspired countless others ever since – not least the folk-singer Bob Dylan. Dylan chose the song 'A Red, Red Rose', written down by Burns in 1794, as the lyric which had the biggest effect on his life.

Timeline

1786/7 In August 1786, the 'Kilmarnock Edition' of poems sold out. It was followed by a revised 'Edinburgh Edition' in April 1787, with an American edition in 1788.

Despite such success and acclaim, Burns remained short of funds. (He found it very difficult to get any money out of his publisher.)

1787 Society for the Abolition of the Slave Trade is formed in London. Scots too were campaigning hard for an end to slavery.

In October, Burns returns to Edinburgh to work with James Johnson on *The Scots Musical Museum.*

An illustration by James M. Scrymgeour of Burns and a friend John Syme, on a later tour in 1793, this time to the Galloway area. A brief stop at Kenmuir Castle, home of John Gordon, Viscount Kenmuir, is said to have inspired Burns to write 'Scots Wha Hae'. When Robert died three years later, John Syme proved to be a great support to Burns' widow and family.

Highland journey

Mystery object

Can you work out what this instrument is and what it might be made of?

It belonged to Burns, who said it 'was made by a man from the Braes of [Atholl], and is exactly what the shepherds [would] use in the country'. Answers on page 40

'… a country where savage streams tumble over savage mountains …' Robert Burns

After his visit to the Borders, Burns set off for the Highlands – again on horseback. This tour was in complete contrast, almost like a visit to a foreign country. Gaelic was spoken, Highland chiefs still held sway over their clans-folk and the landscape was unforgiving. The laws of Edinburgh and London had little effect on the Highlands.

In June 1787 Burns explored the West High-lands, north through Glasgow, past Loch Lomond and west to Inveraray. Here he was invited to visit the Duke of Argyll in his new castle. In August and September, Burns went north via Crieff to Blair Atholl. It was at Blair Castle that he met Niel Gow, the famous fiddler to the Duke of Atholl. Burns was fascinated by Gow's collection of strathspey reels, songs and lyrics.

Blair Castle features in this later book of music arranged by Helen, Lady Forbes. It was dedicated to the Atholl Highlanders, Europe's only lawful private army, reformed in 1839. Such regiments, and their defence of Queen Victoria's Empire, helped to restore national pride, which suffered badly after the Jacobite rebellions. Burns, born in 1759, witnessed the bitter aftermath of the rebellions, which saw the break-up of the Highland way of life.

Background: An engraving of Loch Lomond, with Ben Lomond behind it.

Niel Gow

Niel Gow (1727-1807) was 60 when Burns met him on his Highland tour. Gow played jigs, reels and strathspeys at Highland weddings and balls in the great houses. He was one of the founding fathers of the Scottish fiddle.

Come screw your pins and gie's a screed
Fae your unrivalled fiddle
Nae fabled wizard's wand I trow
Had e'er the magic airt o' Gow
When wi' a wave he draws his bow
Across his wondrous fiddle.

Burns' tribute to Gow
when the musician visited Dumfries

Burns loved history, so he visited many battlefield sites connected to the Jacobites and their rebellions of 1715 and '45. These sites later inspired him to write the songs 'The Battle of Killiecrankie', 'The Battle of Sherramuir' and 'Johnny Cope'. The famous song 'Scots Wha Hae' (also titled 'Robert Bruce's march to Bannockburn') celebrated King Robert I's victory against the English King Edward II in 1314.

On leaving the Highlands, Burns was asked to make a toast at table – which he did, 'much to the pleasure of all who heard him':

When death's Dark stream I ferry o'er,
(A time that surely shall come,)
In Heav'n itself I'll ask no more,
Than just a Highland welcome.

Fashion in Burns' day

Mystery objects

These are everyday objects that were owned by Robert Burns. Do you know what they are and what they might be made from?

Answers on page 40

'Burns, when at home, usually wore a broad blue bonnet, a blue or drab long-tailed coat, corduroy breeches, dark blue stockings and cootikens [woollen leggings]. In cold weather a black and white checked plaid was wrapped round his shoulders.'

William Clark, ploughman at Ellisland

'His dress was perfectly suited to his station, plain and unpretending, with a sufficient attention to neatness. [In Edinburgh] *he always wore boots; and when on more than usual ceremony, buckskin breeches.'*

Dugald Stewart, writer, Ayrshire and Edinburgh

'His black hair, without powder, at a time when it was very generally worn, was tied behind, and spread upon his forehead. … from his person … and dress, had I met him near a seaport … I should have probably [guessed] *him to be the master of a merchant vessel of the most respectable class.'*

Professor Walker, author of a Life of Burns

Clothes for country and city living were worlds apart. In Ayrshire, country people spun their wool and linen thread from their own sheep and flax. A spinning wheel was an essential item in the cottages and farmhouses. The village weaver then made the cloth for clothing and bedding. Clothing was sourced locally and designed to be practical. In winter, Burns' plaid was useful for carrying lambs, and the broad Kilmarnock bonnet kept his head warm.

Country women wore a short jacket over a striped petticoat, protected by a large apron. Women wore a cap if married, but went bare-headed if single. Children wore much the same as the adult style and often went barefoot. If they were lucky enough to have a good set of clothes, these were kept for church on Sunday!

Perfumers in Edinburgh preferred to use bear fat for greasing ladies' and gentlemen's hair! This picture shows some of the more outlandish styles of wigs that were fashionable in Burns' day.

Clothes detective

How many differences can you list between Burns in his country clothes and those worn for the city?

Study all the fabrics of the clothes you are wearing. How many different fabrics can you name? Find out how the cloth is made – is it produced from natural fibres (for example, 100 % cotton)?

List if you can where the clothes were made (the labels will help you).

City clothes were much more elaborate. Ladies wore hooped skirts, amazing hair styles and huge hats. Men wore lace at the neck and cuffs, often with a wig for special occasions, and a tricorn or three-cornered hat for stepping out in the city. Outsize silver buckles on their shoes and a smart walking cane finished off the outfit.

Timeline

1786   David Dale opens a cotton mill at New Lanark on the Clyde. Newly-invented spinning machines driven by water power slowly replaced the hard work of weaving in cottages. Cotton was a cheaper fabric and more adaptable than linen.
Dale was an industrial pioneer, one of the first employers to offer homes to his workers. Children formed a large part of his work force (smaller fingers could handle the threads more easily).

1795   Prime Minister William Pitt puts a tax on hair powder, but his plan is outwitted when people promptly stop wearing wigs!

a musical Souter

Ellisland

'… a ruinous bargain …'

Robert Burns

An early prototype of a steamboat developed by Patrick Miller and William Symington, being tested on Dalswinton Loch in *c*.1788. Miller owned the lease of Burns' farm at Ellisland.

After a second winter in Edinburgh, Burns married Jean Armour and they lived in a tiny room in Mauchline, back in Ayrshire. His wife was not of farming stock and was sent up the road to Mossgiel to learn from her mother-in-law how to work a dairy.

Aged 29, Burns then took on the tenancy of a farm at Ellisland, near Dumfries. It was meant to be a 'bargain' rent and he signed the lease, although the state of the farm did not impress him. The land was totally neglected – old 'run-rig' strips, little drainage, no hedges to keep animals off the crops – and there wasn't even a farmhouse.

However, his wife Jean and infant son Robert moved south from Mauchline, and by May 1789 they were all in a new house – complete with a new Carron range for the kitchen. Their second son Francis was born in August.

Below: Ellisland in more recent times.

Right: A postcard of Tam o' Shanter and Souter Johnnie. Tam's hat gave rise to the name of a woollen bonnet or beret – the 'Tam o' Shanter'.

Knowing that his published work and farming were not enough to support a growing family, Burns became an exciseman in Dumfries. But even two full-time jobs did not deter him from his first love – writing. Any spare time spent travelling was used to work on his songs. He was still assisting James Johnson who was working on later volumes of *The Scots Musical Museum*. 'Auld Lang Syne' – written in 1788 during a time when he was apart from his wife – and 'John Anderson My Jo', were two of his most famous songs, composed while wrestling with farmwork.

By 1790 Burns had been promoted and was able to employ extra farmworkers to help improve his land – but the soil was exhausted and couldn't support enough crops or cattle. It was while still at Ellisland that Burns composed 'Tam o' Shanter: A Tale', a narrative poem of 224 lines written in a single day on the banks of the River Nith. At the end of 1791 Burns sold off all his stock and quit the farm for town life in Dumfries.

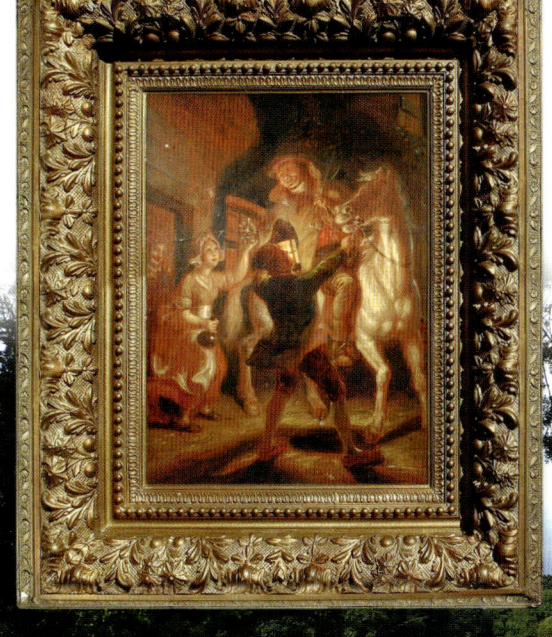

Below: A scene from 'Tam o' Shanter'. Tam leaves the inn on his epic journey home (see pp. 38-39). Behind it is a photograph of the River Nith, where Burns sat down to write the poem.

Timeline

1787/8 First convicts from Britain are sent to Botany Bay, Australia – where Sydney now stands.

1789 The French Revolution. Parisians storm the Bastille prison on 14 July.

George Washington becomes the first President of the United States of America under its new Constitution.

Quick questions

- Burns' landlord at Ellisland was a man called Patrick Miller. He was an inventor preparing for the more industrial age to come. What mode of transport did he develop? (Burns was thought to have been invited for a trip on it!)

- What was the old 'run-rig' system of farming?

- What was the 'new Carron range for the kitchen'? Where was it made?

Answers on page 40

Exciseman in Dumfries

'The Deil's awa wi' th' Exciseman …'

from a song by Robert Burns

Britain's wars abroad were paid for by customs duties on imported goods. Between 1775 and 1815 Britain was at war almost all the time – either with America, or with France.

In Scotland the major goods smuggled were imported tobacco, wine, spirits and tea. Whole families around the Scottish coasts took part in outwitting the Revenue Officers to avoid paying the high duties. Local militia were often called upon to help the excisemen. The centre for prevention in the Solway area was Dumfries.

Burns' first role as an exciseman was hard. His health was failing and he had to ride over 200 miles a week to collect Excise duties, in all kinds of weather. After moving to a three-roomed house in Dumfries with Jean and their three young sons, he was transferred to an Excise district within the town.

Two years later, in 1792, Burns was promoted again, when he was involved in the capture of a smuggling ship, *Rosamund*, stuck on a mud bank. The local Dragoons and Burns himself waded out into the freezing sea to capture the ship.

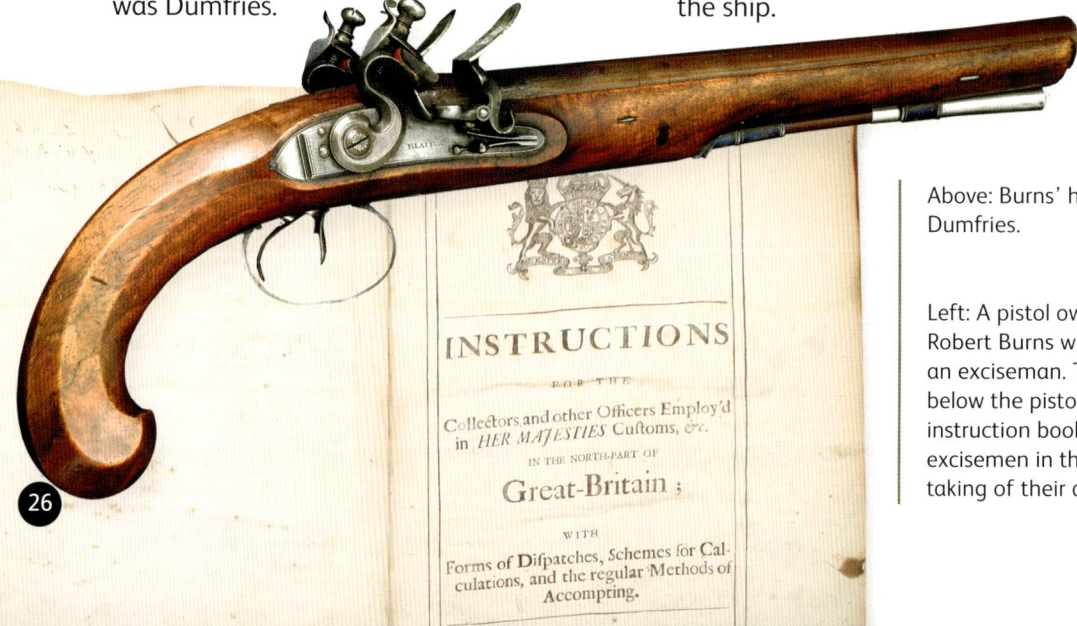

Above: Burns' house at Dumfries.

Left: A pistol owned by Robert Burns when he was an exciseman. The book below the pistol is an instruction book for the excisemen in the undertaking of their duties.

INSTRUCTIONS

FOR THE

Collectors, and other Officers Employ'd in *HER MAJESTIES* Customs, &c.

IN THE NORTH-PART OF

Great-Britain;

WITH

Forms of Dispatches, Schemes for Calculations, and the regular Methods of Accompting.

Burns' poor health did not deter him from voicing support for the French Revolution and he got into trouble from his employer – the Government. However, in 1794, after moving to a larger house, he became Acting Supervisor of the Excise Division of Dumfries. Burns was still writing and composing, but money and health worries were sadly closing in on him. He often had to borrow money, and to add to his troubles his Excise salary was reduced when he was ailing.

Tricks of the trade

Smugglers used to muffle horses' hooves and oil their horses to avoid capture. Hiding places for smuggled goods were often ingenious – fake gravestones, pigsties and concealed cellars were favourites, as well as the many caves on the Solway coast.

Burns the rebel

When the smuggling ship *Rosamund* was later broken up, Burns bought four brass cannons from it and sent them to France in sympathy with the French Revolutionaries. He then had to plead to keep his job, as the Government of the day was not amused.

Above: An Excise permit, signed by Burns, dated 30 November 1793, to allow Thomas Harkness to receive one cask of rum (ten gallons) from John Hutton of Dumfries.

Smuggling off the Solway Coast was a common occurrence. Dumfries Port Division of the Excise extended over the entire estuary of the River Nith from Carsethorn to Glencaple, and included shipping bound for Dumfries.

Her Majesty's Customs and Excise

Now known as HM Revenue and Customs (HMRC), this is one of the oldest Government departments, dating back to Roman times.

Excise duties were not only raised on imported goods; there were also taxes on whisky, bricks, salt, paper, windows – and even, briefly, on hats!

Customs Officers at ports and airports are still trying to beat smugglers in their illegal trade of drugs, guns, wild animals and plants. The officers also work with the Royal Fishery Protection Squad and guard the borders of the United Kingdom.

Funny you should ask …

Questions that are often asked about Robert Burns …

Was Burns a good singer?

He frankly admitted he couldn't sing well, but he had a very good ear for music. Burns only published many of his songs after he had heard them sung by his friend David McCulloch (Wee Davie) – called 'the finest warbler' by Walter Scott.

Did Burns ever wear the kilt?

Never. An Act of 1746 made the wearing of Highland dress illegal, except for soldiers in Highland regiments. There were no 'clan' tartans until the nineteenth century.

Could Burns play the fiddle?

Yes, Burns started to play at age 22. He was able to pick out a tune, as folk songs were sung to him. The fingering on the fiddle helped him to write down the wonderful songs that he heard.

What was his favourite pet?

His collie Luath is often shown in paintings and statues. The poem 'The Twa Dogs' is about Luath and a posh dog called Caesar. Burns also had a soft spot for pet sheep and horses.

Did he only write poems and songs?

No, he also wrote hundreds of letters to friends, family, girlfriends, business contacts, publishers, and people who had been his host. They were all written with great style and on a wide range of subjects. Sending letters in those days was very expensive as the postage rate was based on the distance over which the letter was carried, as well as the number of sheets in the letter.

There was a Penny Post service in Edinburgh in 1777. Letters and parcels could be delivered for one penny to an address within one mile of the Mercat Cross. In 1786 the London to Edinburgh mail coach took 60 hours.

Were there other famous poets in Burns' time?

Yes, there were Gaelic poets, but their work wasn't read by Lowland Scots as few understood the Gaelic language. Burns admired the Edinburgh poet Robert Fergusson's work and donated money for a gravestone to him in Canongate Kirkyard when Fergusson died.

Burns also read the English poets – Samuel Taylor Coleridge was only 13 years younger than him – as well as the works of William Blake, William Cowper and William Wordsworth.

Could we have a Burns' competition at school?

Definitely yes! Organise your own, or as an Enterprise Project. The Burns Federation offers recitation, singing, writing, art, instrumental, choral and project work from Primary 1 through to Secondary stages. Go to: **www.worldburnsclub.com/schools**

How many children did Burns have?

He was father to 12 children by four different women. Burns was fortunate that his wife, Jean Armour, cared for some of the children of his many love affairs in their own home.

'Epistle to a Young Friend'

The following extract is the first and last part of one of the hundreds of letters that Burns wrote. It was sent to Andrew Aiken in May 1786. Andrew was the son of his old friend Robert Aiken, a lawyer in Ayr. Is it a song, sermon, or just wise advice?

I lang hae thought, my youthfu' friend,
A something to have sent you,
Tho' it should serve nae ither end
Than just a kind memento:
But how the subject-theme may gang,
Let time and chance determine:
Perhaps it may turn out a sang;
Perhaps turn out a sermon.

Ye'll try the world soon, my lad;
And, Andrew dear, believe me,
Ye'll find mankind an unco squad,
And muckle they may grieve ye:
For care and trouble set your thought,
Ev'n when your end's attained;
And a' your views may come to nought,
Where ev'ry nerve is strained.

I'll no say, men are villains a':
The real, harden'd wicked,
Wha hae nae check but human law,
Are to a few restricked;
But, och! Mankind are unco weak
An' little to be trusted;
If Self the wavering balance shake,
It's rarely right adjusted!

*   *   *

Adieu, dear, amiable youth!
Your heart can ne'er be wanting!
May prudence, fortitude, and truth,
Erect your brow undaunting!
In ploughman phrase, 'God send you speed,'
Still daily to grow wiser;
And may ye better reck the rede,*
Than ever did th' adviser!

*reck the rede = reckon the counsel or weigh the advice

Sea-bathing in the Solway Firth

'Have you any commands for the other world?'

Burns to his friend, Maria Riddell

In 1793 Britain was at war with France. Local regiments known as militia were formed to protect the country from invasion. Burns joined the Dumfries Volunteers, but to add to his worries the costly uniform and weapons had to be paid for. There was still a huge gulf between rich and poor throughout Scotland, much to the anger of Burns.

In 1795 the harvest failed and the price of oats rocketed. This was followed by three months of famine. In March 1796 there were serious food riots in Dumfries. Just a year before he died, Burns wrote 'A Man's a Man for A' That', a lasting anthem to equality.

Many years of farming toil were taking their toll. Burns had no strength left for another

Brow Well, Dumfriesshire. Spring water was thought to be a cure for ill-health at this time.

volume of poetry. His health was fast failing and some of his friends were deserting him. Medical care was still very limited in those days, and anything and everything was used in the mixing of drugs. Burns' doctor advised sea-bathing in the Solway as a 'cure' for his rheumatic fever. Also recommended was to drink the water at Brow Well, near Ruthven, Dumfries. It was a spring that was thought to have minerals with healing properties.

Burns' last letter was to his father-in-law James Armour in Mauchline, to plead for help for his wife. On 21 July 1796 he died of a heart condition. His last son, Maxwell, was born as Burns' funeral ceremony took place.

Burn's extraordinary energy was finally extinguished, but the memory of the man and his work remains very much alive.

Website watch

Listen to 'A Man's a Man for A' That' at:

www.bbc.co.uk/robertburns

The Burns' songs 'Dumfries Volunteers' and 'Poor and Honest Sodger' became pop-songs of their day, firing up the public imagination.

Timeline

1792	France is proclaimed a Republic.

1792/3 Sir Alexander Mackenzie (born in Stornoway and a Canadian fur-trader) is the first European to cross the Canadian Rocky Mountains to the Pacific Ocean.

1793 The Metric System is introduced in France.

Britain is at war with France.

1796 Mungo Park, Scottish explorer and surgeon, reaches the River Niger.

Edward Jenner gives the first small-pox vaccination.

Robert Burns dies from his heart condition on 21 July, aged 37.

Left and below: The mausoleum to Robert Burns in St Michael's Churchyard, Dumfries is the final resting-place of Robert Burns and Jean Armour.

This statue to Jean Armour is in Dumfries. She was born in Mauchline, Ayrshire, in 1765, and first met Robert in 1784 on a drying green, as she chased his dog away from her laundry! Jean bore him nine children and died 38 years after his death.

JEAN ARMOUR
1765 – 1834
WIFE OF ROBERT BURNS
ERECTED BY
BURNS HOWFF CLUB
SEPTEMBER 2004

Robert Burns the patriot

'A patriot: a person who loves his country and supports its authority and interests; (or) one who exerts himself to promote the well-being of his country.'

Dictionary definition

Title page of the 1822 edition of *Original Scottish Airs for the Voice*, edited by George Thomson, who was assisted by Burns in the assembly of this collection.

Burns was a patriot in various ways. He was a patriotic poet. He wrote many of his best poems in Scots not English. Even in those days, many important Scottish poets, such as Thomas Campbell, William Beattie and James Thomson, were choosing to write in what was becoming standard English. But Burns often chose Scots because he felt most at home with Scots. His schooling did not take him as far as secondary education. Maybe that was just as well, because it meant that no one tried to 'educate' him away from Scots into using English. Such an experience could have killed his poetry dead.

Burns was also a passionate collector of Scottish songs and poetry by other people. In the 18th century, lots of these songs were not yet written down; so by travelling up and down the country, he met local poets, songwriters and musicians, and noted their work down in writing. Burns had huge enthusiasm

and skill for this work. In this he resembled Sir Walter Scott, who some years later also noted down the local literature of his native land. But Scott was a wealthy man, he had a good job as a lawyer and could afford such a hobby. Burns, on the other hand, was a far-from-wealthy farmer and exciseman who could ill afford hobbies – but that did not hold him back.

Much of the subject matter of Burns' poetry was Scottish. Flush with his early success, where did Burns choose to travel? As we have seen, he left Ayrshire to visit Edinburgh, the Borders and through the Central Belt to the Highlands – hence poems and songs like 'Address to Edinburgh', 'Scots Wha Hae', and 'My Heart's in the Highlands'. It is interesting, however, that he did not embark on a tour of England. Burns, it appears, was a very Scottish rather than British patriot.

Scottish patriots

Other Scottish patriots were warriors, such as **William Wallace** and **Robert the Bruce**, who fought Scotland's corner on the battle-field. Robert Burns was a poet patriot – he fought her corner on the printed page. He was a man of the people. He wrote rather disrespectfully about the king, George III, and was sympathetic to the principles of the French Revolution. His democratic intellect strikes a chord with one strong strand of Scottish history – think of the **Declaration of Arbroath** (pictured above, and see page 7).

The statue of Robert Burns in Dumfries was first unveiled by the Earl of Rosebery on 6 April 1882. It was based on a model put forward by the artist Amelia Paton Hill, who was known for her work on portraits and animal figures.

33

Favourite quotations

Opposite: This lithograph (1859) by Maclure & Sons marks the centenary of the birth of Robert Burns. Based on a portrait for the centenary by Sir Daniel Macnee FRSA, it contains scenes from the life and poems of Burns. The scenes include 'Scots Wha Hae', 'The Twa Dogs', 'Tam o' Shanter', the Burns Cottage and the Burns Monument.

'I like to have quotations ready for every occasion ...'

Burns, in a letter to Clarinda

Then gently scan your brother man,
Still gentler sister woman;
Tho' they may gang a kennin wrang,
To step aside is human ...

from 'Address to the Unco Guid'

But facts are chiels that winna ding,
An' downa be disputed ...   'A Dream'

Had we never lov'd sae kindly,
Had we never lov'd sae blindly,
Never met – or never parted,
We had ne'er been broken-hearted.

'Ae Fond Kiss', written to Clarinda

John Anderson my jo, John,
When we were first acquent,
Your locks were like the raven,
Your bonny brow was brent.

'John Anderson My Jo'

Scots, wha hae wi' Wallace bled,
Scots, wham Bruce has aften led,
Welcome to your gory bed,
Or to Victorie!   'Scots Wha Hae'

But pleasures are like poppies spread,
You seize the flow'r, its bloom is shed;
Or like the snow falls in the river,
A moment white – then melts for ever ...

'Tam o' Shanter'

O wad some Pow'r the giftie gie us
To see oursels as ithers see us!
It wad frae mony a blunder free us,
An' foolish notion ...   'To a Louse'

Wee, sleekit, cowrin', tim'rous beastie,
O, what a panic's in thy breastie!
Thou need na start awa sae hasty,
Wi' bickering brattle!   'To a Mouse'

The best laid schemes o' mice an' men
Gang aft a-gley.   'To a Mouse'

Then let us pray that come it may,
(As come it will for a' that,)
That Sense and Worth o'er a' the earth,
Shall bear the gree, an' a' that.
For a' that, and a' that,
It's comin' yet for a' that,
That Man to Man, the warld o'er
Shall brithers be for a' that.

'A Man's a Man for A' That'

The world's legacy

'When Scotland forgets Burns, then history will forget Scotland ...'

J. S. Blackie, Scottish scholar

Only a few years after Burns' death, a copy of his Collected Poems was as common in Scottish households as the Bible. His work has now been translated into many languages. 'Auld Lang Syne' has been adopted by the Chinese, Japanese and Russians to celebrate events. 'A Man's a Man for A' That' is now known as the world's anthem – the song that has come down to us through the years as a prayer and a prophecy. Thousands of overseas visitors still throng to the Burns Country to see the famous sites and soak up the atmosphere. Where else can you find a street called Auld Nick's View, referring of course to the Devil in some of Burns' poems?

There are over 200 statues, memorials and monuments to Burns in Scotland and around the world. Wherever Scots expatriates gather together, Burns Clubs have been formed. In 2009, to commemorate 250 years since Burns was born, a record-breaking Burns Supper evening was held simultaneously, all the way from Argentina to Sri Lanka!

At one time every library in America funded by the entrepreneur Andrew Carnegie was given a bust of Robert Burns. The 16th President of the United States of America, Abraham Lincoln (1809-65), could recite 'Tam o' Shanter' by heart and dreamt of visiting Burns' birthplace in Alloway – 'if I can contrive to cross the Atlantic'.

The Robert Burns Humanitarian Award is given to anyone – any gender, age or creed – if it can be shown that they have enriched the lives of others. How could Burns possibly have foreseen such worldwide fame? He had the common touch, yet managed to capture the soul of Scotland and the world. Little wonder that we pay such tribute to his work.

AULD NICK'S VIEW

The first major celebration of Robert Burns was held in 1844, the 85th anniversary of his birth, timed so that his three sons could attend. Although this took place in Alloway, other events began to spring up. At Mauchline in 1896, a replica of a wooden plough used in Burns' time was carried through the village on a horse-drawn cart in celebration of the life of the poet.

Suffragette story

Frances Mary Parker (1875-1924) was the niece of Lord Horatio Kitchener, and a prominent member of the militant wing of the Scottish Women's Suffrage movement. Imprisoned many times for her actions in support of women's right to vote, she is particularly well known for attempting to set fire to the Burns Cottage in Alloway in July 1914, along with fellow campaigner Ethel Moorhead. Although Moorhead escaped, Parker was arrested and brutally force-fed in prison when she went on hunger-strike. The First World War prevented Parker from further campaigning and she served courageously in the Women's Army Auxiliary Corps. She was later awarded the Order of the British Empire.

Tam o' Shanter: A Tale

'Tam o' Shanter' is one of Burns' best loved poems. Read the whole work to enjoy the atmosphere and the build-up of suspense. The following extracts will whet your appetite.

… As Tammie glowr'd, amaz'd and curious,
The mirth and fun grew fast and furious:
The piper loud and louder blew,
The dancers quick and quicker flew.
They reel'd, they set, they cross'd, they cleekit,[1]
Till ilka carlin swat[2] and reekit,
And coost her duddies[3] to the wark,
And linket at it in her sark![4]

       *   *   *

Tam tint[5] his reason a' thegither
And roars out, 'Weel done, Cutty-sark!'[6]
And in an instant all was dark.

Opposite and below: Etchings of original sepia drawings, dated 1855, by John Faed of scenes from 'Tam o' Shanter'. The poem is said to have been influenced by the vivid tales of Betty Davidson, an older relative of Burns who was a source of many of his imaginative writings (see page 4). 'Tam o' Shanter' was written for a new publishing venture being compiled by Francis Grose (pictured opposite). Grose was an antiquarian and a friend of Burns.

The Poem

'Tam o' Shanter: A Tale' was written in one day, at Ellisland in the autumn and early winter of 1790, when Burns was 31 years old. He was said to have been highly entertained during the writing of his text, bursting into laughter at frequent intervals!

Fast facts

- Alloway Kirk only ceased to be used for public worship in 1756.
- Burns' father was buried in Alloway Kirkyard in 1784.
- From the Kirkyard gate to the 'key-stane' of the Brig o' Doon is only 400 metres.

*   *   *

Ah, Tam! Ah, Tam! thou'll get thy fairin',[7]
In hell they'll roast thee like a herrin'!
In vain thy Kate awaits thy comin',
Kate soon will be a woefu' woman!
Now, do thy speedy utmost, Meg,
And win the key-stane of the brig.
There, at them thou thy tail may toss,
A running stream they dare na cross.
But ere the key-stane[8] she could make,
The fient a[9] tail she had to shake!
For Nannie, far before the rest,
Hard upon noble Maggie prest
And flew at Tam wi furious ettle;[10]
But little wist she Maggie's mettle!
Ae spring brought off her master hale
But left behind her ain grey tail:
The carlin claught[11] her by the rump
And left poor Maggie scarce a stump …

Glossary

1. cleekit = linked hands
2. carlin = witch; swat = sweated
3. coost = cast aside; duddies = clothes
4. sark = vest
5. tint = took leave of
6. Cutty-sark = short shift
7. fairin' = just deserts
8. key-stane = mid-stone
9. fient a = never a
10. ettle = effort
11. claught = clutched

Francis Grose, c.1790

Below: John Faed's drawing of Nannie in her sark (shirt) leaping to catch hold of Meg's tail before she gets to the 'key-stane' of the Brig o' Doon.

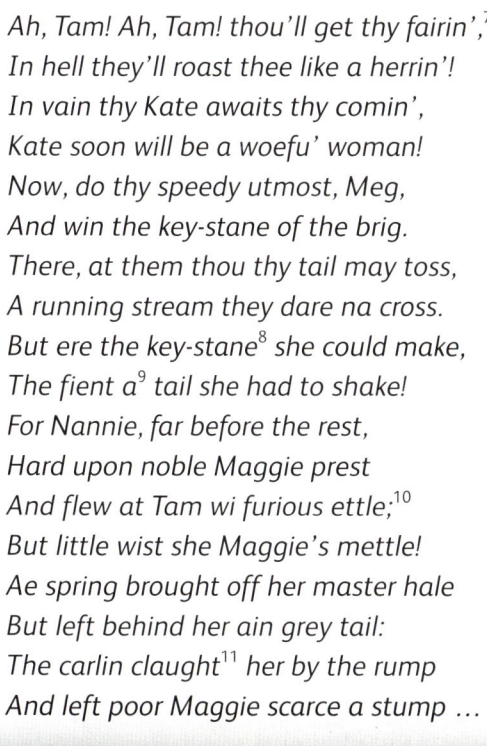

ANSWERS

Page 14: Mystery objects – Venetian glass beads such as these examples (*c.*1780) were often used as barter at slave markets on the west coast of Africa.

Page 19: Route finder – Burns may have seen Dunbar Castle, Jedburgh Abbey and Melrose Abbey, among many other landmarks. See what else you can find.

Page 20: Mystery object – A 'chanter', part of a 'stock-and-horn' or pastoral pipe made out of bone, which belonged to Robert Burns.

Page 21: Modern-day Scottish fiddlers – Aly Bain, Charlie Cowie, Alistair McCulloch, Aidan O'Rourke.

Page 22: Mystery objects – These are buttons owned by Robert Burns. They are made from agate. Agate was thought to protect against the 'evil eye'.

Page 25: Quick questions – Patrick Miller developed a steamboat with William Symington (see p. 24).

– The old 'run-rig' system of farming was the division of land into narrow arable strips. 'Runs' were the furrows; 'rigs' were the ridges of earth.

– The Carron range (see p. 5) was a stove with a cooker attached. It was made in an iron foundry near Falkirk, which also made agricultural and other products that required iron castings. Carron Ironworks once operated its own fleet of steamships and even issued its own currency for its global trade.

Facts and activities section

Page iii: Fast facts – Mount Aconcagua is 6962m above sea level and is the highest mountain in the Americas.

Page iv: Word search – Answers below.

Page iv: Criss-crossword – Answers: (1) Dumfries; (2) Saturday; (3) Clarinda; (4) Georgia; (5) Agnes; (6) porridge; (7) Gow; (8) Jamaica; (9) wee

Page v: Famous Scots – Answers: 1=F, 2=C, 3=E, 4=B, 5=A, 6=D

USEFUL WEBSITES

BBC – for Declaration of Arbroath, Industrial Revolution and material on Robert Burns

www.bbc.co.uk/history/scottishhistory/media_museum

Burns Country – for poem texts and encyclopaedia

www.robertburns.org

Dumfries Museum – for material on the time of Robert Burns

www.futuremuseum.co.uk

Learning and Teaching Scotland – for farming in the 1700s, and information on the Slave Trade

www.ltscotland.org.uk/scottishhistory/industrialrevolution/daily life

Music in Scotland –

www.musicinscotland.com

The National Burns Collection – Burns database

www.burnsscotland.com

National Library of Scotland – for Burns' background and legacy

www.nls.ac.uk

National Maritime Museum – for Slave Trade information

www.nmm.ac.uk

National Museums Scotland – for National Museum of Scotland and National Museum of Rural Life

www.nms.ac.uk

National Trust for Scotland – for Burns' Cottage

www.nts.org.uk

Scottish National Portrait Gallery –

www.nationalgalleries.org.uk

Wikipedia –

www.wikipedia.org

World Burns Club – for Burns Quiz and Learning Resources

www.worldburnsclub.com/schools

FURTHER READING

– The Poems of Robert Burns. Many editions are available, including good second-hand copies.

– *Scottish Folk and Fairy Tales from Burns to Buchan* (Penguin Classics, 2008).

Robert Burns
in Time and Place

Facts and activities

This book belongs to:

_____

Write your name on the above line.

A celebration: Burns' Night

The Origins of the Supper

Robert Burns and his male friends often met in a tavern or public house in Ayrshire, to drink, debate, argue and sing songs after a busy day on their farms or place of work. When people wanted to honour the memory of Robert Burns after his death, they followed the traditions set down by groups such as Burns' Tarbolton Bachelors' Club, and from such beginnings the world-famous Burns Night celebration emerged.

Burns' Nights are held by Scots at home and by Burns' clubs abroad – from Australia, Canada, China, Russia to the United States of America. The poet's work has touched the world. A Burns Supper celebrates the birthday of Robert Burns on 25 January 1759.

You will need ...

To hold your own Burns Supper, make a list of those who will sing, recite a poem, or make a short speech, and someone to act as a chairperson.

You will also need:

- A haggis
- Tatties (potatoes)
- Neeps (turnip)
- A soft drink to toast your guests
- A copy of Burns' poems

Instructions

Plan your programme very carefully – make sure there are some funny elements, as well as serious ones.

Organise some Burns music CDs, or people who can play Burns' music on the pipes or fiddle.

Programme of events

- When the haggis is piped in, it is placed in front of the person who has been chosen to recite the **Address to the Haggis**.

- **The Selkirk Grace** is then spoken by the chairperson and the haggis is served with tatties and neeps. This is the main item on the menu. (Remember to keep some of your soft drink for the toasts that follow.)

- The main speech is now given. It could be about some aspect of the life of Robert Burns or a theme related to the poet's work. This main speech leads up to the toast to **The Immortal Memory of Robert Burns**.

- The toast **To the Lassies** is proposed by a boy and replied to by a girl. Keep the toast light-hearted. Between toasts there can be recitations or songs.

- After a vote of thanks by the chairperson, everyone sings **Auld Lang Syne**. Try to learn the chorus and the first and last verses. This song is very useful to sing at ceilidhs, Hogmanay and lots of other celebrations. The words were adapted by Robert Burns from a traditional song.

Auld Lang Syne

Should auld acquaintance be forgot,
And never brought to mind?
Should auld acquaintance be forgot,
For auld lang syne!*   *times gone by

CHORUS
For auld lang syne, my dear,
For auld lang syne,
We'll tak a cup o' kindness yet,
For auld lang syne.

And there's a hand my
   trusty fiere*   *friend
And gie's a hand of thine,
And we'll tak a richt gude
   willie waught*   *goodwill drink
For auld lang syne.

Website

If you need more inspiration, go to:

www.scotland.org/burnsnight/interactive

Fast facts

- 'Auld Lang Syne' is played in Japanese supermarkets to tell customers that it is closing time.
- The highest Burns Supper thus far recorded was held in 2007 at the top of Mount Aconcagua in Argentina by Chris Dunlop, the Scottish mountaineer. Can you find out how far above sea level this is?

Answer on page 40

Puzzles!

Word search

There are 20 words below related to the poetry and life of Robert Burns. They are hidden in this word square. Can you find them? You can move diagonally, as well as up and down, in any direction, to find the words:

Answers on page 40

N	H	S	B	S	E	W	A	R	B	G	A	L	L
J	A	A	I	I	L	P	W	S	G	C	M	E	U
Y	R	M	G	G	L	E	M	C	Q	S	A	I	A
D	Y	G	E	O	G	R	E	U	H	G	T	G	T
H	A	F	U	S	D	A	A	K	K	B	L	S	H
M	C	G	U	H	I	I	H	T	I	G	I	S	A
S	H	H	X	M	N	C	C	B	C	T	S	O	R
R	N	C	I	T	C	Y	X	A	O	G	U	M	E
M	T	C	A	I	A	D	N	E	U	N	P	X	T
M	O	N	H	W	E	I	S	N	O	S	P	Y	U
A	C	U	O	C	R	E	E	C	H	B	E	X	O
E	W	L	S	N	D	D	B	D	K	F	R	O	S
T	L	T	H	E	Q	A	L	A	S	S	I	E	S
A	K	C	O	N	R	A	M	L	I	K	H	F	J

ACQUAINTANCE
ALLOWAY
BARD
BRAW
CREECH
EXCISEMAN
HAGGIS
KILMARNOCK

LASSIES
LUATH
MAGGIE
MOUSE
MOSSGIEL
PLOUGH
SLEEKIT
SONSIE

SOUTER
SUPPER
TAM
TWA

Criss-crossword

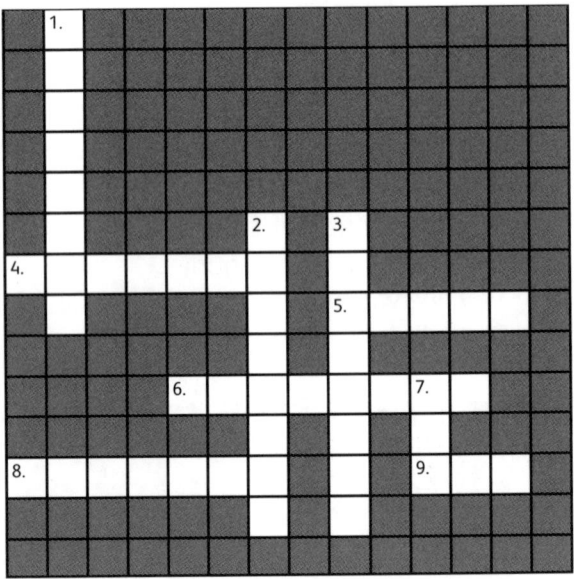

Answer the following questions to complete this word puzzle:

1. Burns became an exciseman in this Scottish town. (See pp. 26-27)
2. 'The Cotter's _____ night.' (See pp. 8-9)
3. Burns wrote 'Ae Fond Kiss' for this lady. (See pp. 16-17)
4. A replica of Burns' birthplace is in this American state. (See pp. 4-5)
5. First name of Burns' mother. (See pp. 4-5)
6. A very healthy breakfast. (See pp. 8-9)
7. Surname of a famous fiddler. (See pp. 20-21)
8. Burns almost emigrated here. (See pp. 14-15)
9. The first word of the poem 'To a Mouse'. (See pp. 34-35)

Answers on page 40

Famous Scots

Scotland during the 18th century and into the 19th century was full of people who contributed their talents to the period of the Enlightenment. Can you match these famous Scots to their inventions or talents?

Which Scot …

1. … worked out a Theory about how the Earth was formed?

2. … wrote poems, plays and songs, including 'The Gentle Shepherd'?

3. … was the designer of the 'Comet' paddlesteamer and organised the first successful steamboat service in Europe?

4. … was a mechanical engineer and inventor whose version of the Newcomen engine made a huge contribution to the Industrial Revolution?

5. … is now referred to as the Father of Modern Economics?

6. … was a professor of chemistry and medicine who worked on the principles of heat and carbon dioxide?

Answers on page 40

Adam Smith

James Watt

Allan Ramsay

Joseph Black

Henry Bell

James Hutton

Tam o' Shanter's scary adventure

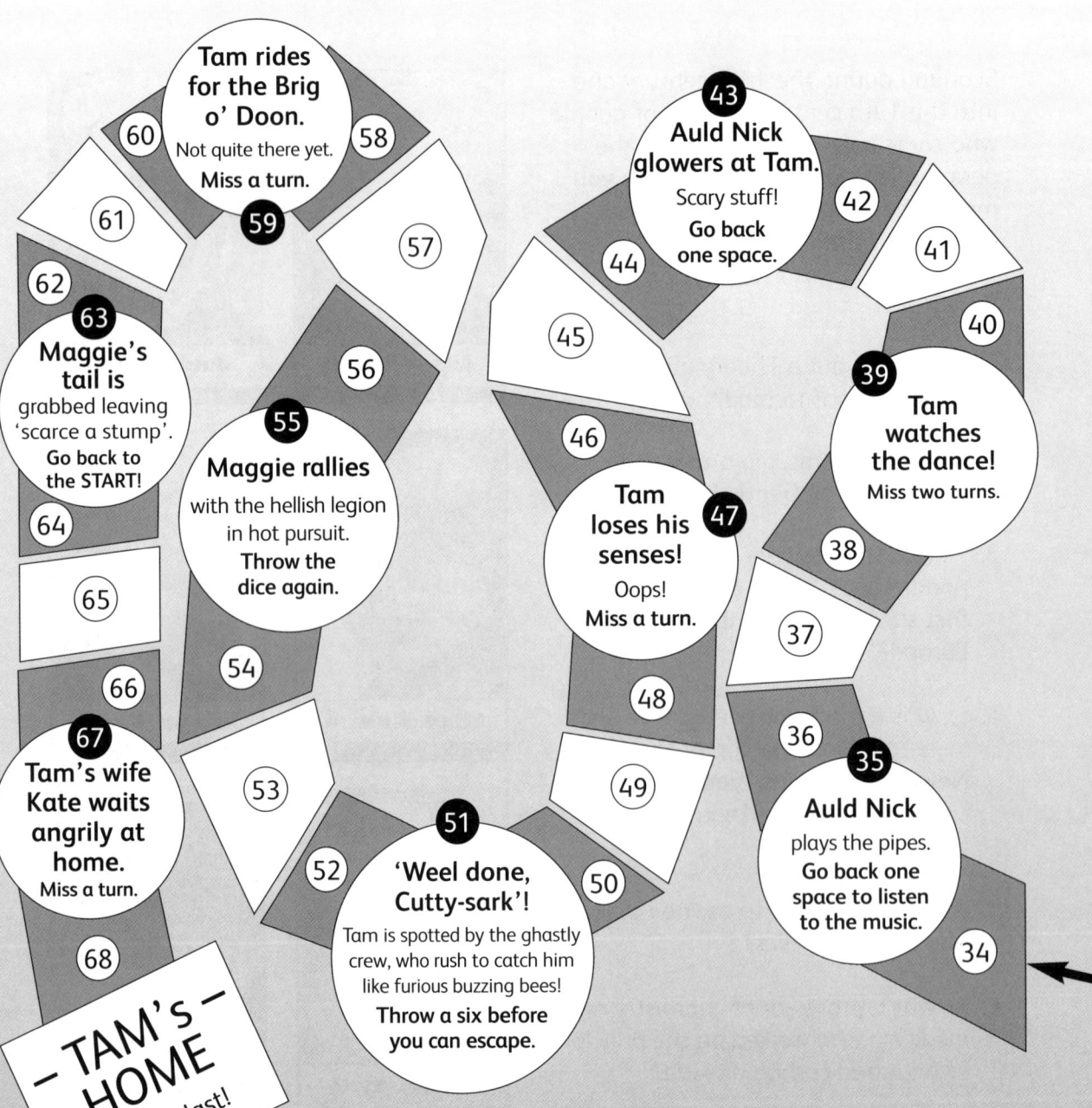

This is a game for 2 to 4 players. You will need a dice. You will also need a small counter for each player. Follow the instructions on the spaces you land on.

To move, throw the dice.

The winner is the player who reaches home first!

23 Crossing River Doon!
Avoids falling in.
Move forward one space.

22

24

25

21

26

20

27 Kirk Alloway
Maggie the mare halts 'sair astonished' at 'unco sight'!
Miss a turn.

19 Heading for Kirk Alloway
No bogles to 'catch him unawares'!
Throw the dice again.

28

18

17

29

16

30

31

33 Warlocks and witches
in jigs and reels!
Miss a turn to stare.

32

– START –
THE INN

1

2

3 Kirkton Jean
prophesies Tam will drown!
Miss a turn.

4

5

6

15 Stormy weather!
Tam heads for home through 'rattlin' showers'!
Miss a turn.

14

13

12

11

10

9

8

7 Souter Johnny
and Tam get fou!
Throw the dice again.

vii

PLACES OF INTEREST

Here is a list of places to visit which have connections with Robert Burns. As opening times in these places may vary, it would be useful to check the details with the local Tourist Information Office.

AYRSHIRE

ALLOWAY
- Burns National Heritage Park
- Burns Cottage and Museum, Burns Monument (1823) and gardens, Kirk Alloway and Brig o' Doon (National Trust for Scotland)
- Robert Burns Birthplace Museum (open 2010)

AYR
- Tam o' Shanter Inn (High Street)
- Auld Kirk (where Burns was baptised), River Ayr and Auld Brig (River Ayr Walk)

KILMARNOCK
- Dean Castle Country Park

KIRKOSWALD
- Souter Johnnie's House, Main Road

MAUCHLINE
- Burns House Museum and Mossgiel (1 mile away)

TARBOLTON
- Bachelors' Club (National Trust for Scotland)

DUMFRIESSHIRE

DUMFRIES
- Burns House and Mausoleum
- Dumfries Museum
- Ellisland Farm
- Robert Burns Centre

EDINBURGH
- The Writers' Museum
- High Street/Royal Mile
- National Museums Scotland
- Scottish National Portrait Gallery

GREENOCK
- HM Customs and Excise, Greenock Customs House

NEW LANARK
- Conservation Village and Visitor Centre

WESTER KITTOCHSIDE
near EAST KILBRIDE
- National Museum of Rural Life (National Museums Scotland)

FURTHER CREDITS